HOW TO DRAW

CRASH

BANDICOOT™ AND FRIENDS

BY RON ZALME

UNIVERSAL©

UNIVERSAL
INTERACTIVE STUDIOS

www.universalstudios.com

Troll

Special thanks to Cindy Chang

A Creative Media Applications Production

Art Direction by Fabia Wargin Design

Published by Troll Communications L.L.C.
ISBN 0-8167-5634-1
10 9 8 7 6

INTRODUCTION

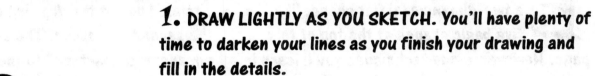

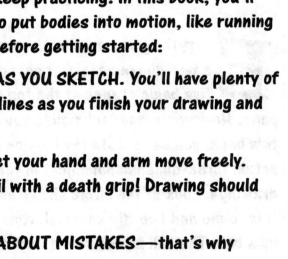

CRASH BANDICOOT™ here, welcoming you to this awesome book! Get ready for some high-speed action and amazing fun. In this easy-to-use book, you'll learn how to draw me, as well as my sister, Coco™. You'll also learn how to draw a bunch of bad guys like Dr. N. Brio™, Dr. Neo Cortex™, Koala Kong™, Komodo Moe™ & Komodo Joe™, Dr. N. Gin™, Papu Papu™, Pinstripe Poteroo™, and Tiny the Tiger™. In no time, you'll be making your own outrageous drawings and creating brand-new Crash Bandicoot™ adventures.

Don't worry if your drawings aren't perfect the first time. Keep practicing! In this book, you'll learn how to draw facial expressions, and you'll learn how to put bodies into motion, like running and jumping. Here are a couple of things you should know before getting started:

1. DRAW LIGHTLY AS YOU SKETCH. You'll have plenty of time to darken your lines as you finish your drawing and fill in the details.

2. STAY LOOSE! Let your hand and arm move freely. Don't grip your pencil with a death grip! Drawing should be fun and relaxing.

3. DON'T WORRY ABOUT MISTAKES—that's why erasers were invented!

4. PRACTICE, AND BE PATIENT. It takes time to get good at drawing. So grab your pencil and get started. I'm outta here. See ya!

3

BASIC SHAPES

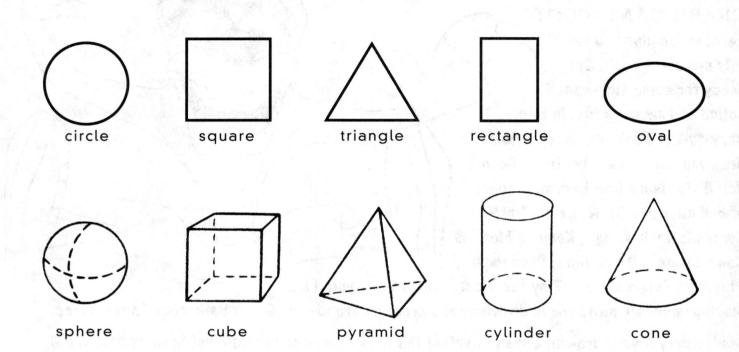

circle   square   triangle   rectangle   oval

sphere   cube   pyramid   cylinder   cone

Everything you draw with your pencil is a two-dimensional flat shape, like the five basic shapes at the top of this page. However, using techniques you'll learn in this book, you can create the illusion of an actual three-dimensional object in your drawings. Look at the circle shown above. It is round and two-dimensional. Now pick up a ball. The ball is also round, but it is three-dimensional, an actual object. The trick to drawing believable characters is to create the illusion on paper that what you are drawing is three-dimensional (like the ball), even though it is really only two-dimensional (like the circle). Look at the drawing of the sphere in the second row above. The sphere is the three-dimensional "partner" to the circle. You can see that just by adding the two crisscrossing dotted lines to the drawing of the circle, you can create the illusion of the three-dimensional sphere. The same can be done with each of the shapes shown on this page. Practice drawing the two-dimensional shapes, then work on the 3-D shapes like the cube, pyramid, etc. After you've practiced for a while, you'll be ready to start drawing Crash!

CRASH BANDICOOT ™

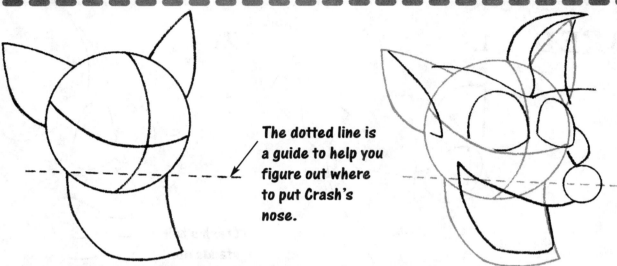

The dotted line is a guide to help you figure out where to put Crash's nose.

1. Start with a circle to form Crash's head. Make it look like a sphere by drawing a curved line that goes from left to right across the circle, and another from top to bottom. These are known as "crosshairs." They help show the direction Crash is facing and how his head is tilted. Next, add the ears and jaw, as shown. Lightly draw a straight dotted line near the bottom of the circle.

2. Add the eyes, mouth, and nose, and more details on the ears. Once you've drawn the nose circle, erase the dotted line.

3. Now add details to Crash's eyes, eyebrows, nose, mouth, and hair. Begin the upper and lower teeth.

4. Blacken Crash's eyes, eyebrows, nose, and mouth. White highlights on the eyes and nose help give them a realistic gleam. Add vertical lines to show his teeth. Erase the crosshairs and any extra lines. Congratulations—you're off to a great start!

CRASH BANDICOOT™

SCARED

1.

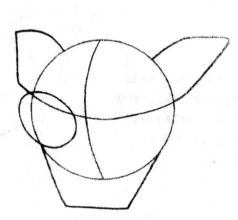

2.

Crash's hair stands up.

DETERMINED

Start with an oval shape instead of a circle.

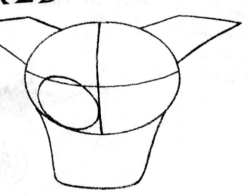

HAPPY

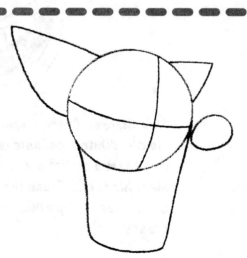

In order to give Crash facial expressions, you need to start by drawing his head. Follow the steps on page 5 to start Crash's head. Then add the details below to complete each of the three expressions shown here.

3.

Crash's eyebrows angle down, his eyes are wide open and tall, his teeth are clenched together, and his mouth is turned down.

4.

Crash's eyebrows angle up, his eyes are rounder, his teeth are clenched together, and his mouth is turned up at the corners.

Crash's mouth is wide open, with lots of space between his upper and lower teeth. His upper lip turns up, like a smile.

CRASH BANDICOOT™

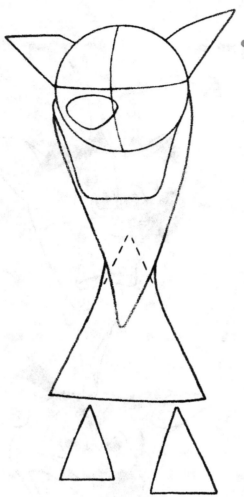

1. Start the full body of Crash Bandicoot by drawing the head circle. Add the crosshairs and the nose. His upper body is a long, curved triangle that starts and ends on the sides of the head circle. His legs are formed by another triangle (pointed up). His ankles also start as triangles. Begin the ears and mouth, as shown.

2. Next, add Crash's arms, hands, and legs. Start with straight lines just to get the position. You can smooth them out later. Add two half-circles for his sneakers, overlapping the ankle triangles. Begin the hair and eyes, and add detail to his ears, mouth, and chest, as shown.

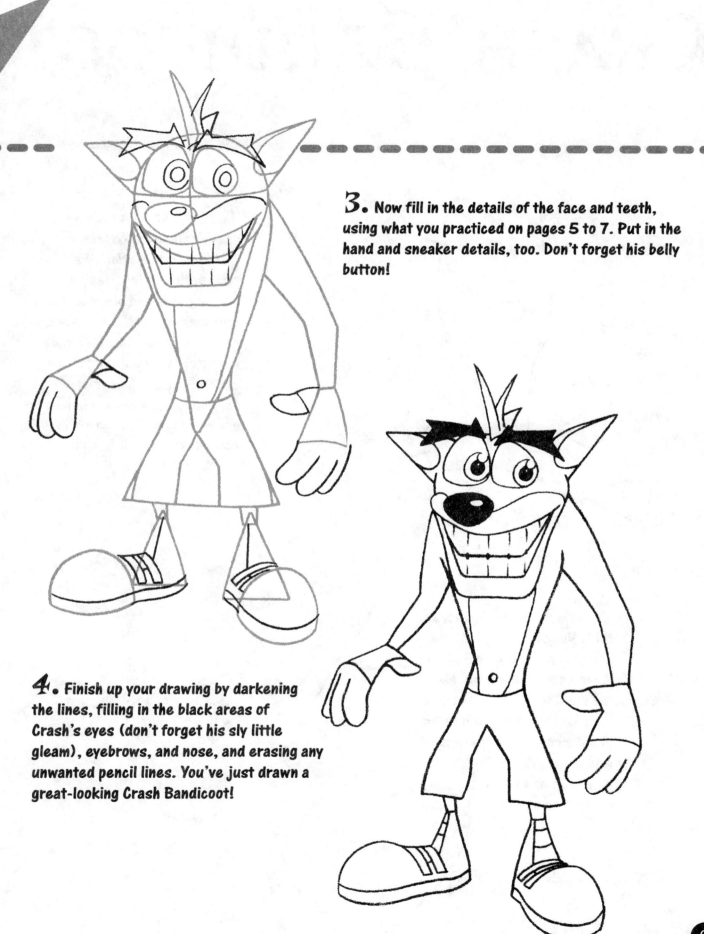

3. Now fill in the details of the face and teeth, using what you practiced on pages 5 to 7. Put in the hand and sneaker details, too. Don't forget his belly button!

4. Finish up your drawing by darkening the lines, filling in the black areas of Crash's eyes (don't forget his sly little gleam), eyebrows, and nose, and erasing any unwanted pencil lines. You've just drawn a great-looking Crash Bandicoot!

CRASH BANDICOOT™
Running

1. Now that you've drawn Crash's whole body, let's put that body into motion. We'll start with running. Begin by drawing the head circle and crosshairs. Add the ear, nose, and chin. Draw the upper body triangle, but make the bottom square, rather than pointy. For the running pose, the legs are rectangles that go off to the sides.

2. Add the arms, hands, and feet. Notice the angle of the arms. They appear to be pumping as Crash runs. Make the front foot (his left) bigger than his back foot, so it looks like it's coming right at you. Add some hair, the eyes and inner ear, and body details, as shown.

3. Fill in details like the eyebrows, face, fingers, sneakers, and belly button. Round off some of the sharp angles (like the arms).

4. Finally, blacken the eyebrows, eyes, nose, and mouth. Erase any unwanted lines. To make Crash look like he is really zooming, add some speed lines behind him!

11

CRASH BANDICOOT™
Jumping

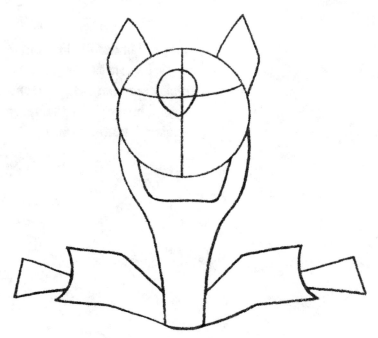

1. Making Crash jump is similar to making him run. The biggest difference is that in the jumping pose, he is facing forward.

2. Add his arms, and draw triangles for the position of the hands. Notice how they are tilted in this pose. Draw his feet, then add hair, inner ears, eyes, mouth, and body details, as shown.

3. Next, add the fingers, sneakers, and more details on the face and body, as you have done before.

4. Fill in the black parts (eyes, eyebrows, nose, and mouth), clean up your lines, and watch Crash Bandicoot jump!

COCO BANDICOOT™

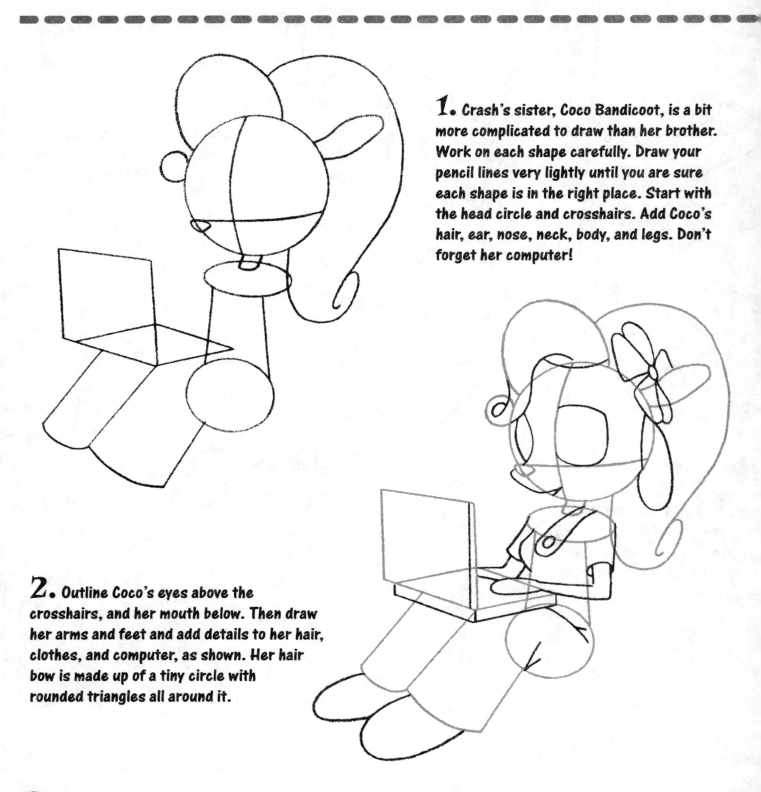

1. Crash's sister, Coco Bandicoot, is a bit more complicated to draw than her brother. Work on each shape carefully. Draw your pencil lines very lightly until you are sure each shape is in the right place. Start with the head circle and crosshairs. Add Coco's hair, ear, nose, neck, body, and legs. Don't forget her computer!

2. Outline Coco's eyes above the crosshairs, and her mouth below. Then draw her arms and feet and add details to her hair, clothes, and computer, as shown. Her hair bow is made up of a tiny circle with rounded triangles all around it.

3. Continue adding details, as shown, including Coco's eyelashes, eyebrow, and eyes. Draw her fingers on the keyboard, and the bottoms of her shoes.

4. Fill in the black areas (eyebrows, eyes, and nose), and add her eye highlights. Erase any extra lines, and you've got a terrific Coco Bandicoot!

Dr. N. Brio™

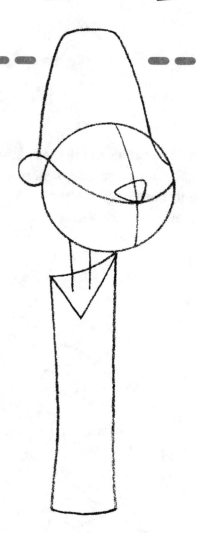

1. No adventure is complete without a few nasty bad guys. Let's learn how to draw some of them, starting with Dr. N. Brio. Begin with the basic head circle and crosshairs. Place the doctor's triangle-shaped nose just above the point where the crosshairs meet. Draw his ear and neck, then add a rounded rectangle to the top of the circle to complete the shape of his long head. Draw a long, narrow rectangle with a triangle at the top for his body.

2. Next, draw Dr. N. Brio's eyes, eyebrows, jaw, and lower lip (that's the lip that helps make him look so mean). Begin the bolts on his head. Use the basic triangle shape to form his shoulders and the laboratory beakers, and connect them with rectangular shapes for his arms and hands. Don't forget to include his feet.

3. Complete his fingers and ears and the bolts on his head, and add the remaining details, as shown.

4. Fill in the black areas (eyes, thick eyebrows, inside of his sleeve). Add some bubbles and smoke to Dr. N. Brio's evil concoctions, erase any extra lines, and you've drawn a truly mad scientist!

DR. NEO CORTEX™

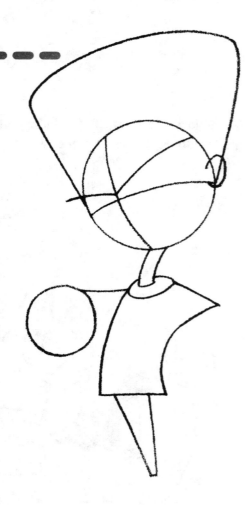

1. While we're on the subject of doctors, let's learn how to draw Dr. Neo Cortex. Start, as usual, with the head circle and crosshairs. Angle the eyebrow lines above the crosshairs. Add an ear and the large, curved rectangular shape shown to create the outline for Dr. Neo Cortex's head. Draw the body, as shown. Notice the curve on the right side of the body shape. Add a circle, which will become the top of his right glove, and connect it to the body with a straight line.

2. Begin the left arm and glove and both hands. Outline the feet. Then add the doctor's wacky hair. Don't worry if the hair you draw doesn't match the hair shown. Make his eyebrows bushy by adding lots of little lines at the ends. Draw his eyes, nose, and mouth, and on his forehead, make the square shape that will become the letter "N."

3. Draw his fingers and his beard and add details to his feet, body, and face, as shown. Finish the letter "N" by adding little triangles to the square.

4. Fill in the black areas—his hair, eyebrows, beard, arms, and legs—erase any extra lines, and the doctor is in!

KOALA KONG™

1. Next up in our parade of baddies is Koala Kong. Start with a small head circle and position the crosshairs so they meet very high on the circle. Place a kidney-bean shape over the circle, and add a nose and two round ears. Make Koala Kong's chest big. Use circles to create his arms, and rectangles for his wrists and hands. Add the legs, as shown.

2. Next, draw Koala Kong's angry eyes and snarling mouth. Soften the outline of his furry ears, and add a tuft of hair. Add some more lines, as shown, to give shape to his arms and hands. Begin his feet, and draw his T-shirt and belt.

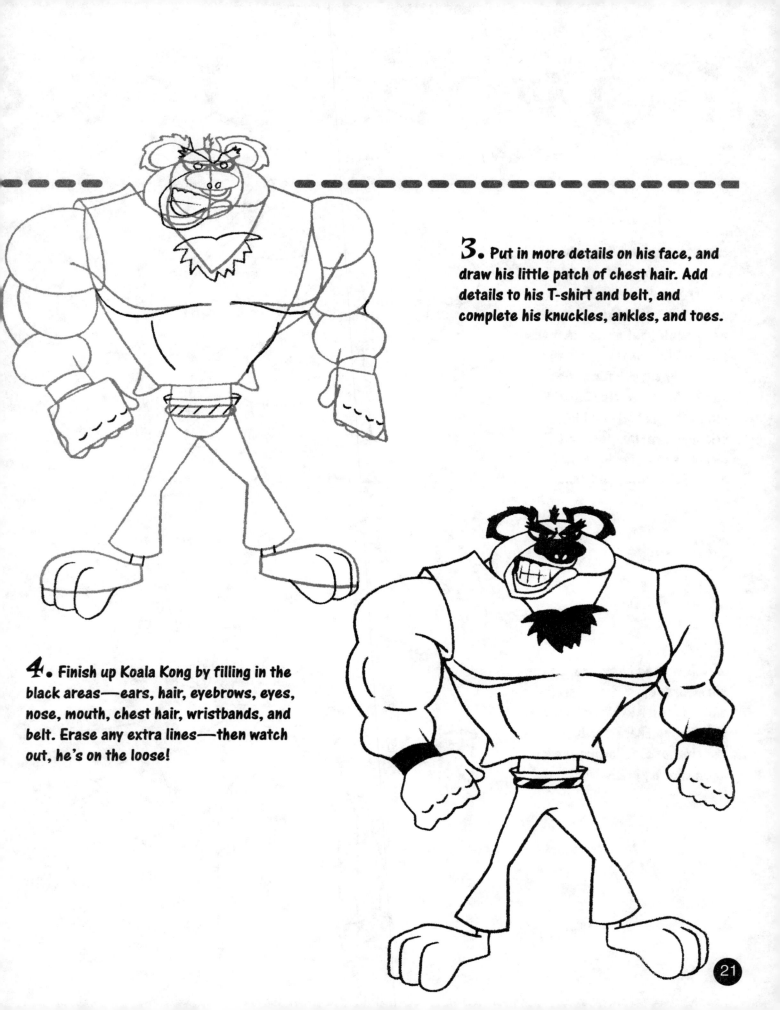

3. Put in more details on his face, and draw his little patch of chest hair. Add details to his T-shirt and belt, and complete his knuckles, ankles, and toes.

4. Finish up Koala Kong by filling in the black areas—ears, hair, eyebrows, eyes, nose, mouth, chest hair, wristbands, and belt. Erase any extra lines—then watch out, he's on the loose!

21

1. Start by drawing only Moe (or Joe, if you prefer). It'll be easier to add the second character behind him. Draw the head circle, but notice that the left-to-right crosshair is wavy. This will help you form Moe's (or Joe's) brow. Use a big circle for his body and the triangles, rectangles, and circles shown for his mouth, arms, legs, feet, and hands.

2. Draw the basic shapes for his sword, eyes, mouth, robe, and fingers. At this point, start the second character behind the first one, following the lines shown here.

KOMODO MOE™

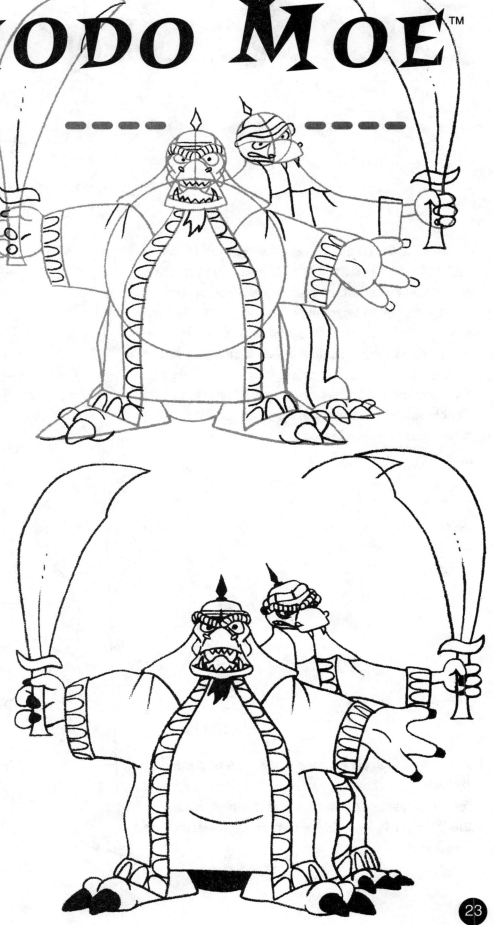

3. Now it's time for details. For both Moe and Joe, add toes, fingernails, teeth, eyes, and helmets. Give the front figure a beard and the rear figure a sword. Then draw the squiggly patterns on their robes, and add details to the robes and swords, as shown.

4. Fill in all the black areas shown on Moe, then do the same for Joe. Erase extra pencil lines, and you've got a matched set of fearsome warriors!

DR. N. GIN ™

1. Next is Dr. N. Gin (try saying that ten times fast!). Dr. N. Gin's head is different from the heads of the other characters you've practiced so far. Start with two overlapping ovals. Draw one line from the top of the top oval to the bottom of the bottom oval to form your crosshairs. Add a circle on the left side, where the ovals overlap. Use a third, larger oval to make his body. Draw a triangle for his collar, a rectangle for the bomb in his head, and two skinny rectangles to make his legs.

2. Begin to draw his face and hair. Add details to the bomb, as shown. Then draw his arms, two cones for his gloves, and two rectangles for his hands. Don't forget to include his feet and the small circles on his body.

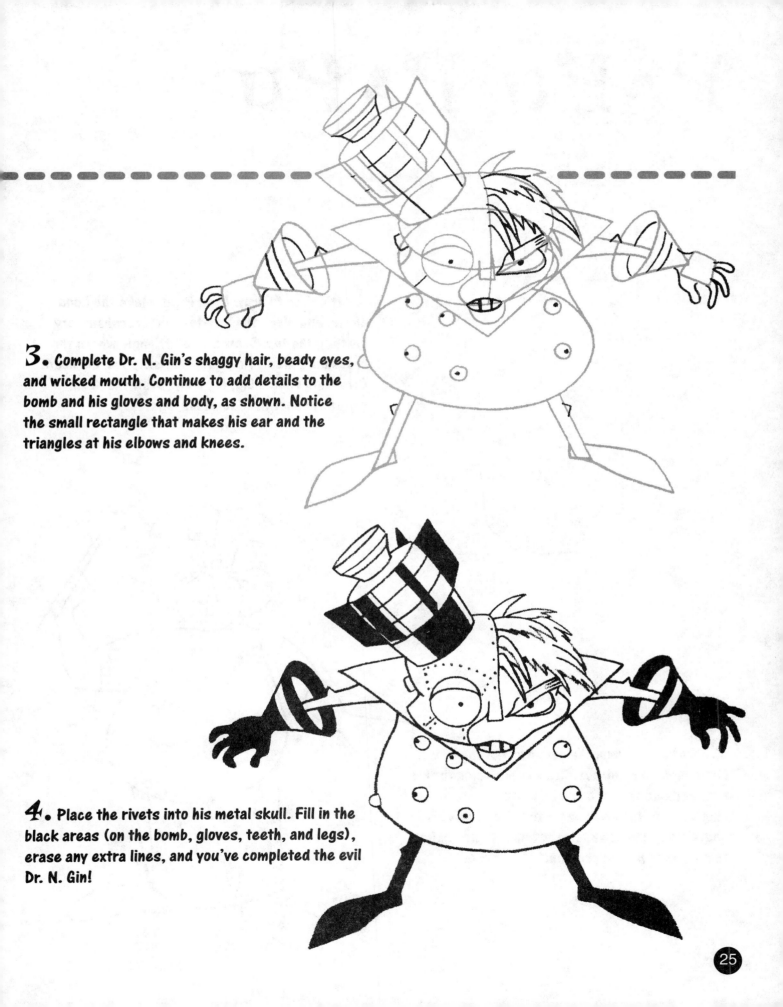

3. Complete Dr. N. Gin's shaggy hair, beady eyes, and wicked mouth. Continue to add details to the bomb and his gloves and body, as shown. Notice the small rectangle that makes his ear and the triangles at his elbows and knees.

4. Place the rivets into his metal skull. Fill in the black areas (on the bomb, gloves, teeth, and legs), erase any extra lines, and you've completed the evil Dr. N. Gin!

PaPu PaPu ™

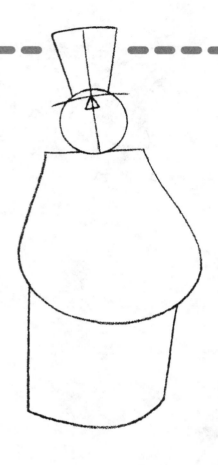

1. It's time to draw Papu Papu. Make the head circle, and place the left-to-right crosshair very close to the top. Draw a small triangle where the crosshairs meet. Add a top-hat shape on his head. Give Papu Papu a big, big belly. Draw the drum shape, as shown, to form his legs.

2. Outline an umbrella shape at the top of Papu Papu's headdress. Draw semicircles for his hair, and add the face and headdress details, as shown. Draw his arms and wand. Next, add his feet and the up-and-down, zigzag lines on his "skirt." Don't forget his bellybutton!

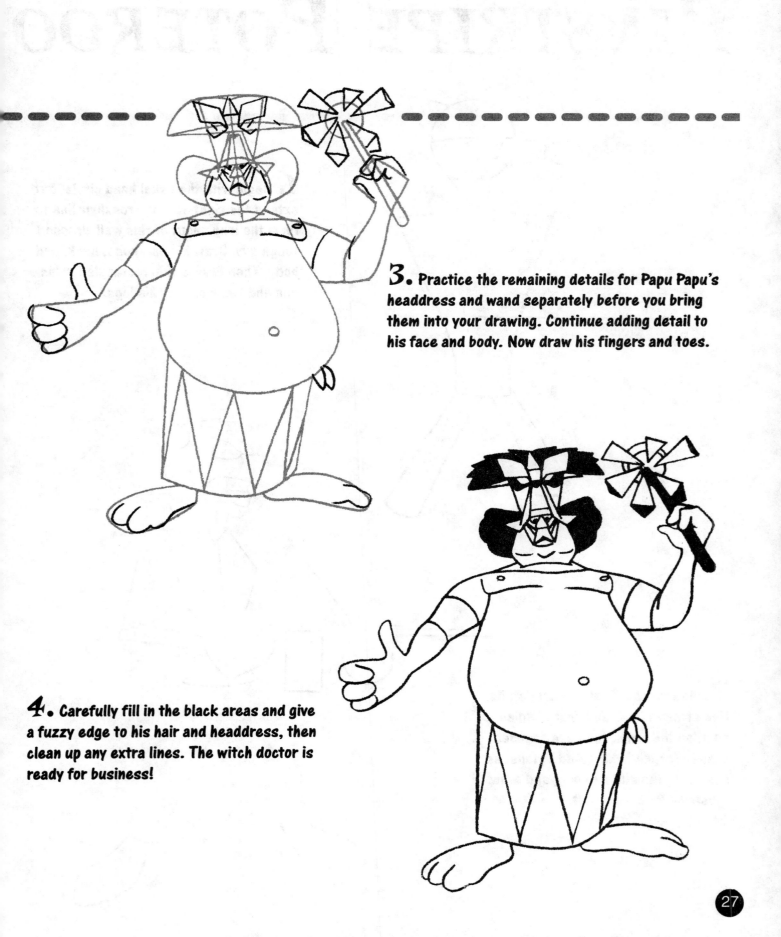

3. Practice the remaining details for Papu Papu's headdress and wand separately before you bring them into your drawing. Continue adding detail to his face and body. Now draw his fingers and toes.

4. Carefully fill in the black areas and give a fuzzy edge to his hair and headdress, then clean up any extra lines. The witch doctor is ready for business!

PINSTRIPE POTEROO™

1. Begin with the usual head circle, but extend the right-to-left crosshair line to form the long snout of this well-dressed tough guy. Draw his ear, nose, neck, and body. Then draw a thin rectangle for his gun and two more for his legs.

2. Add some hair and facial details. Use straight lines and sharp angles to position the arms, then use rounded shapes for the hands. Add details, as shown, to the suit and gun, and draw Pinstripe Poteroo's feet.

3. Continue adding details to his face, suit, and gun. Draw his fingers, and complete his boots.

4. Finally, fill in the black areas—leaving white highlights in the shoes, as shown, to make them look shiny. Erase any extra lines you have drawn. Told you Pinstripe Poteroo was well dressed!

TINY THE TIGER™

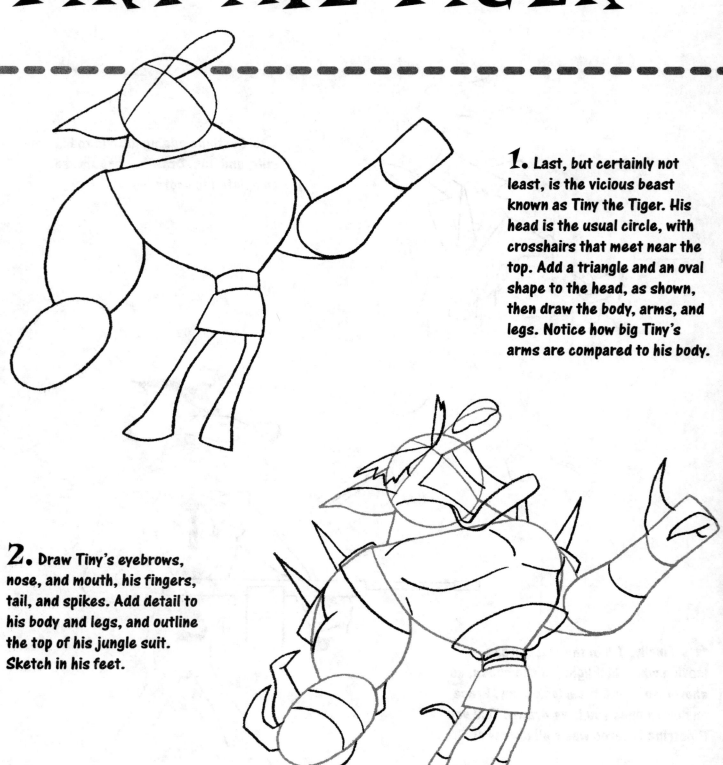

1. Last, but certainly not least, is the vicious beast known as Tiny the Tiger. His head is the usual circle, with crosshairs that meet near the top. Add a triangle and an oval shape to the head, as shown, then draw the body, arms, and legs. Notice how big Tiny's arms are compared to his body.

2. Draw Tiny's eyebrows, nose, and mouth, his fingers, tail, and spikes. Add detail to his body and legs, and outline the top of his jungle suit. Sketch in his feet.

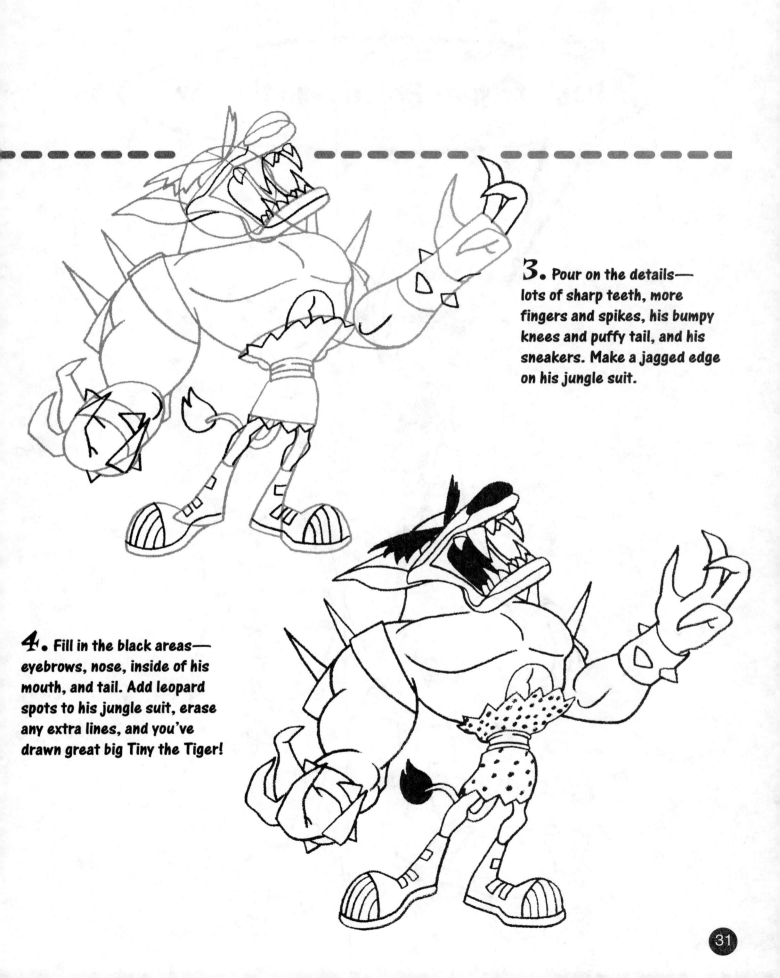

3. Pour on the details— lots of sharp teeth, more fingers and spikes, his bumpy knees and puffy tail, and his sneakers. Make a jagged edge on his jungle suit.

4. Fill in the black areas— eyebrows, nose, inside of his mouth, and tail. Add leopard spots to his jungle suit, erase any extra lines, and you've drawn great big Tiny the Tiger!